Teenage Refugees From

CAMBODIA

Speak Out

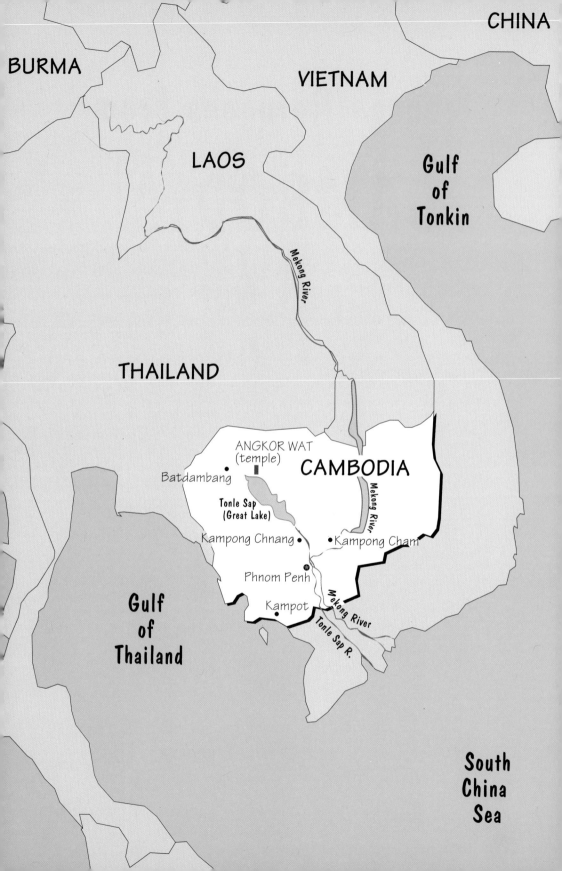

CHINA

BURMA

VIETNAM

LAOS

Gulf
of
Tonkin

Mekong River

THAILAND

ANGKOR WAT
(temple)

Batdambang

CAMBODIA

Mekong River

Tonle Sap
(Great Lake)

Kampong Chnang

Kampong Cham

Phnom Penh

Gulf
of
Thailand

Kampot

Mekong River

Tonle Sap R.

South
China
Sea

IN THEIR OWN VOICES

Teenage Refugees From

CAMBODIA

Speak Out

STEPHANIE ST. PIERRE

THE ROSEN PUBLISHING GROUP, INC.
NEW YORK

Published in 1995 by The Rosen Publishing Group, Inc.
29 East 21st Street, New York, NY 10010

First Edition
Copyright © 1995 by The Rosen Publishing Group, Inc.

Manufactured in the United States of America.

Library of Congress Cataloging-in-Publication Data

St. Pierre, Stephanie.
  Teenage refugees from Cambodia speak out / Stephanie St. Pierre. — 1st ed.
    p.   cm. — (In their own voices)
  Includes bibliographical references and index.
  ISBN 0-8239-1848-3
  1. Cambodian American teenagers—Juvenile literature. 2. Refugees—United
States—Juvenile literature. I. Title. II. Series.
E184.K45T45 1995
973'.049593—dc20   94-41411
                                                                          CIP
                                                                          AC

Contents

There are many reminders in Cambodia of the terror and destruction that once took place. A teenage employee at the Museum of Genocide replaces a skull in a display showing thousands of skulls of people killed by Pol Pot and the Khmer Rouge regime.

INTRODUCTION

Cambodia is a tropical country located in Southeast Asia in the Indochinese peninsula. It covers an area about twice as big as the state of Missouri. The unusual geography of the country has much to do with the way it has evolved over time. The center of the country is scooped out like a huge bowl, which is a flood plain. The Tonle Sap (also called the Great Lake) is just about in the center of the plain. The Mekong River and the Tonle Sap River flow through the Great Lake. As the seasons change, the flow of the rivers switches and the waters of the Tonle Sap either recede, draining the plain dry, or overflow, flooding the plain. The central plateau is surrounded by grassy plains and mountain chains heavy with forests.

បុរាណ បណ្ឌិត បានពោលថា ៖ វិជ្ជា នាំ ឲ្យ មាន វិន័យ
វិន័យ នាំឲ្យ មាន សេចក្ដី ថ្កុំថ្កើ សេចក្ដី ថ្កុំថ្កើ នាំឲ្យ បាន
ប្រព្យ សម្បត្តិ ប្រព្យ សម្បត្តិ នាំ ឲ្យ បាន ធមិ ធមិ ដឹកនាំ
ឲ្យ បាន សុខ

ENGLISH TRANSLATION FROM CAMBODIAN:
Education leads to discipline; discipline
leads to respect; respect leads to wealth;
wealth leads to karma; and karma leads
to happiness.

Cambodia has two seasons, dictated by the
monsoons that affect climate in Southeast Asia.
Winter lasts from November to May and is cold
and dry. The rice harvest is gathered throughout
Cambodia in December and January, the height of
the "cold" season. Summer lasts from June to
October and is very hot and extremely wet. In late
April the rains begin. This is also the time when
Cambodians celebrate New Year. Throughout the
rainy season the pattern is for heavy rain to fall for
a few hours every evening. By the end of the rainy

During the rainy season, roads are often flooded. People turn to boats for transportation.

season Cambodia is flooded and the rice fields, under a foot of water, are in perfect condition for their crops to mature. Most houses are built on stilts so that the rising water does not flood them, but roads are often washed away, making travel and communication difficult.

Khmer is the national language. Eighty percent of the population are Khmer. Minority peoples make up the other 20 percent of the population. The total population of Cambodia in 1990 was estimated at 7.3 million people, almost the same as in 1962 when the last census was taken. Many deaths and emigrations from the country during prolonged and brutal civil wars account for the lack of growth in three decades.

For thousands of years Cambodians lived quiet, peaceful lives as rice farmers and fishermen. Most Cambodians practiced Buddhism, a religion that prohibits its followers from killing animals or eating meat. It stresses a nonviolent, cooperative way of life. Buffalo and oxen were used as beasts of burden, helping to plow fields, pull carts, and lend their strength to other heavy labor; however, they were almost never used as a food source. People lived in small family groups called *phum,* sometimes not even large enough to be considered villages. Everyone, mothers, fathers, and children, worked the land together. The land was rich, and food was plentiful. During the dry winter months after the rice was harvested, Cambodians spent their time sewing, weaving straw mats, repairing tools, mending their homes, and making things they could use during the rest of the year.

Before 1960 the few cities in Cambodia were small, heavily populated by Vietnamese, Chinese, and Europeans. Many of these people considered themselves Cambodian, though they were not Khmer people, descendants of the ancient people of Cambodia.

Before the wars that ravaged the country throughout the 1970s and '80s, the capital city of Phnom Penh (also the largest city in Cambodia) had a population of only about 200,000. At that time, most

Many Buddhist temples in Cambodia were built in the twelfth century and are found in Angkor.

Cambodians lived on the outskirts of cities and in the fertile countryside. In the 1960s city life became more popular, but most Cambodians still preferred the simple, predictable lifestyle of the small rural farming communities. Rice was still the most important crop, and its cultivation was the focus of the lives of millions of people.

The wars that raged through Cambodia from the 1970s on stemmed from 1863, when Cambodia agreed to what would turn out to be a colonial relationship with France. In 1941, France installed Norodom Sihanouk as King of Cambodia. However, the people of Cambodia wanted freedom

Pol Pot instituted a rule of terror.

from France along with other political and social
reforms. France, believing that it could maintain
control because of having chosen Cambodia's
leader, granted the country its independence in
1953. To keep Cambodia independent, Sihanouk
turned the throne over to his father in 1955, although he himself was elected head of state, and
therefore retained ultimate control, in 1960.

Although Sihanouk intended to concentrate on
modernizing his country, he was drawn into the
conflict between Cambodia's neighbors, North
and South Vietnam. He thought he was minimizing

Cambodia's involvement by breaking away from the Southeast Asia Treaty (SEATO), breaking relations with democratic South Vietnam and its ally the United States, accepting military aid from Communist China, and allowing North Vietnam the use of his country's ports to sustain their Communist forces fighting in South Vietnam. However, these moves would serve only to put Cambodia in the center of action.

It was at this time that a new Communist group called the Khmer Rouge, led by a man named Pol Pot, began growing in Cambodia. In 1968 the Khmer Rouge began an armed struggle to take over the Cambodian government.

In 1969, the United States, which supported South Vietnam, began bombing North Vietnamese bases in Cambodia. By 1970, the U.S., along with South Vietnam, launched an attack to wipe the bases out completely. This devastated the land and people of Cambodia.

The people of Cambodia ultimately suffered horrible losses. As the various wars involving the United States, North and South Vietnam, Cambodia's own government, and the Khmer Rouge raged through the countryside, people lost everything from their homes to their lives. Though their country had seen many wars in its long history, little had so affected every aspect of Cambodian life as when the Khmer Rouge marched into Phnom Penh on April 17, 1975. Many Cambodians looked forward to the end of the wars that had destroyed

The sight of soldiers brought relief to some Cambodians, fear and dread to others.

their country. Some even cheered as Pol Pot's con-
quering armies marched into town. Sihanouk was
exiled.

Pol Pot established a new Communist government
in Cambodia, now called Democratic Kampuchea, or
DK. Thus began his terrifying reign. Based on his inter-
pretation of the Communist ideal, Pol Pot's vision
for Cambodia was a completely agrarian society—
everyone was to farm the land. Pol Pot abolished
the use of money and markets were closed. From
1976 to 1978, cities were emptied as the Khmer
Rouge forced millions of people to the countryside, where they were made to work on collective

The people of Cambodia survived the trauma of a ruthless, destructive government.

Despite the brutal happenings around them, Cambodians managed to maintain their traditional culture. Here a Khmer dancer puts the finishing touches on his costume.

farms as laborers. Mass starvation, exhaustion, malnutrition, and frequent executions killed hundreds of thousands of people. Death was the penalty for disobeying orders, or even for revealing an education or middle-class status. The Khmer Rouge did its best to isolate Cambodia from all other countries. It is estimated that between one and three million people were killed. The sites of those farms are now called the killing fields. As a result of this devastation, a tremendous wave of people fled to refugee camps in Thailand.

Fights to establish the border between Cambodia and Vietnam ended in a Vietnamese invasion of

Phnom Penh in January 1979. Pol Pot and other DK leaders fled to Thailand. The Vietnamese founded a new government called the People's Republic of Kampuchea, which gained popularity with Cambodians through the 1980s. However, food was still scarce, services were nearly nonexistent, and many people were still leaving the country. In the early 1980s, at least 325,000 Cambodians were living in refugee camps in Thailand.

Meanwhile, the Khmer Rouge had began guerrilla resistance against Vietnamese troops. In 1982, Sihanouk joined the Khmer Rouge to create a government in exile to fight for Cambodia's independence. The United Nations (U.N.) extended its support by setting up refugee camps to aid the thousands of Cambodians in need of food and safety.

By 1983 the Vietnamese began withdrawing troops from Cambodia, a process that was not completed until 1989. Cambodia was left to rebuild itself. The people had a long way to go and faced many problems. Many Cambodians lived in fear that Pol Pot, often compared to Hitler, might return to power, despite the fact that he had been found guilty of war crimes and was sentenced to death.

In 1990, the U.N. created a peace plan for Cambodia. In October 1991, Sianhouk was named head of a temporary Cambodian government consisting of four groups, including the Khmer Rouge, although the puppet government was still in place.

Small, rural farming communities were once the ideal lifestyle. Today they are nearly nonexistent as people move to the cities in search of a means of survival.

Arrangements were made to hold an independent election to establish a new democratic Cambodian government. The U.N. kept the peace between the various groups, repatriated hundreds of thousands of refugees, and organized and supervised the elections. More than 90 percent of registered voters participated in the vote. The occupation of more than 20 percent of the country's land by the Khmer Rouge was declared illegal, and Sihanouk was restored to the throne on September 24, 1993. Cambodia was finally independent once again.

Today Cambodia is a very poor country. Children go hungry. Medicine is not available to treat

Efforts are being made to repair the damage done to many of the cultural artifacts of Cambodia, such as these stone carvings in one of the temples at Angkor.

diseases. Roads have fallen into disrepair, and there is no money to fix them. In many ways the country has moved backward in time. Clean water, electricity, communications, and travel have become rare. Many Cambodians who once lived a quiet, happy life in the fertile countryside are now living in urban slums. Civil war continues to threaten the hope of a peaceful time of rebuilding.

Efforts are being made to reestablish the educational system and reduce illiteracy. Important cultural areas that were nearly destroyed by the DK are being revived. Indian archaeologists and Cambodians are working to repair damage done

Angkor Wat, once a glorious temple, was severely damaged by the Khmer Rouge. The current government is making efforts to restore the temple to its original spendor.

to the ruins of Angkor Wat. The National Ballet has recruited and trained new dancers. Cambodian theater, arts and crafts, and literature are also encouraged by foreign and domestic interests.

What does the future hold for Cambodia? No one is quite sure. And so, many Cambodians have chosen to take the uncertain road of the refugee, leaving their homeland in the hope of making a better life for themselves and their families in another country until the day—if it ever comes—that Cambodia can become home again.

*　　　*　　　*

The teenagers interviewed for this book asked that their photographs not be used. In all cases, we have used only the students' first name in order to protect their privacy.◆

Angkor Wat

Angkor Wat is the largest religious building in the world. It was built by King Suryavarman II in the twelfth century AD, over 800 years ago. The city of Angkor was a city of temples, reservoirs, and palaces, home to royalty and the priestly caste during one of Cambodia's most awesome periods. Angkor Wat is a temple dedicated to the Hindu god Vishnu and is thought to have been built as a tomb for Suryavarman II. The entire structure, nearly ten miles long, is surrounded by a moat 200 yards wide. Five towers rise up from the building, representing Mount Meru, the home of the Hindu gods.

The temple is covered with intricately carved bas-relief sculpture that depicts the stories of Hindu gods and the exploits of the King. It was probably painted white on the inside and gilded on the outside, making it glitter on the mountaintop where it is perched. The temple also may have served as an astronomical observatory. Recent discoveries show that the temple structures are aligned with important positions of the sun, moon, and stars.

During the Pol Pot years, Angkor Wat and the other temples at Angkor were neglected. Many scholars worried that the temple itself might have been badly damaged during those years as well. In fact, the temples were not badly harmed, although they had become overgrown with vegetation. Many statues were missing, however. Some of these were moved and stored away by Pol Pot's regime. Others were simply stolen and taken out of the country.

Cambodia is rich in its architectural heritage. Here a soldier guards an ancient temple that has been ravaged by time and thieves.

Tithra, nineteen, has been in North America since 1986. He has spent a lot of time as a gang member with other Cambodian teens in the area where he lives. He wants to be an artist using traditional Cambodian arts and crafts. He would like to return to Cambodia, especially to see the temple of Angkor Wat.

TITHRA
LUCKY TO BE ALIVE

When my family came to the United States, I was eleven years old. First we went to Chicago, where my dad went to school. Then we moved to Boston. We lived there for a couple of years until my father got a different job and we moved to Providence, Rhode Island. There are a lot of other Cambodians living here in Providence. It's not such a big place, not like Chicago or Boston, so it's easier to meet other Cambodians. There are a bunch of women who do Cambodian sewing together.

The kids hang out together. The gangs are mostly a way for us to be with other people who can understand, who have the same kind of background. Our families are pretty strict, so maybe some of the kids go wild when they get old enough to get out of the house. I did for a while, but now I've calmed down a lot. I have plans.

Being in a gang was a way to feel that I wasn't so different from other kids in school. I never fit in at all. I think it was because I was so old when I got here. I learned English pretty good, but I didn't like to talk, join in. I didn't know anything about music or movies and stuff that other kids were interested in. I was no good in sports. I have a younger sister, and I'd spend a lot of time looking out for her too. Kids teased her all the time. She was even worse than me, so shy. Maybe because we lived in too many different places—Thailand, Chicago, then Boston, then Providence—it didn't feel like home until I found other Cambodian kids and we just stuck together.

We had to leave Cambodia because my grandfather was some big soldier on the side that lost. When the Khmer Rouge came to Phnom Penh we had to run away. They killed my grandfather and two of my uncles. They would have killed our whole family.

We had to go through the jungle. I was a little kid. For a while we stayed in Cambodia, in the country, then the soldiers started finding people and making them go to work on these farms all over the place. Sometimes they just killed people. They took my older

Many Cambodian refugees fled to Thailand, a neighboring country. Camps were set up along the border to house the thousands of refugees.

brother for the army. We never saw him after that.

That was when we went into the jungle and then we got to the camps in Thailand. We had to walk most of the way there from Cambodia. We were in Thailand for years. It took a long time to get permission to come to the United States. We had to learn English and learn about American culture. There were rules about everything. Then we finally got to come to the United States and we went to Chicago.

I want to go back to Cambodia. I want to be an artist, to tell people about my own Cambodian

Many young men who were recruited into the Khmer Rouge's army disappeared.
Their families still have no idea whether they are alive or dead.

history. If I can get back to my country, I'll go to the ruins in Angkor. Lots of Cambodian art and stuff was destroyed by the Khmer Rouge and all the wars, but some of it is still there. Also, I'd like to try to find my brother. He might still be alive, but he wouldn't know where we are so he couldn't find us in the United States. Maybe he's dead. I don't know. There were some other relatives from my mother's family but I don't know them at all. They were farmers. I don't think their village exists anymore, so who knows what happened to them? So I'm glad we came to the U.S., even if it isn't perfect. We are still alive.◆

Youeth lives in New York City with her parents and grandparents. She has had a difficult time adjusting to life in North America since she arrived in 1988. She has been responsible for caring for her elderly grandparents and parents, and this has made it hard for her to spend much time away from home learning English and about the customs of the U.S. Despite this, she has learned to speak English quite well and hopes to find a job doing housekeeping or child care. Her life has been very difficult, but she is looking forward to the future.

YOUETH
SOLDIERS TOOK ME AWAY

left Cambodia when I was nine years old. Before the war our family had a simple life as farmers. The war was very bad. Then afterward, the whole country was terrible. Soldiers took me away from my family. I had to live with other children who were taken from their families too. We had to work very hard in the fields. Lots of us got sick. We were so hungry all the time. I was very homesick. I missed my family so much.

One time I tried to run away—to go back to my family. It was at night. When I was running through the streets I saw people killed. The soldiers cut the people's throats and left them dying in the street. It was like in the movie *The Killing Fields.*

Thousands of skulls were found at the "killing fields" in Choeung Ek, one site at which the brutality of Pol Pot's regime was evident. The skulls are on display at different museums throughout Cambodia to remind people of the horrors that can occur.

I was very scared. The soldiers chased me and caught me. They took me back. They told me that if I tried to run away again I would end up like the people they killed. I didn't run away again.

So many people were dying all the time—they just piled up the bodies in the street. I had an uncle in the army who died.

When I went back to my parents, we left Cambodia. That was around 1983. There was no reason to stay. My whole family, my grandparents, parents, and brothers, all left together. We walked for a long

time into the mountains, then we went in a truck

Children were often separated from their parents either by force or by death. Some wound up living in orphanages. Others were forced to work in fields planting and harvesting food.

the rest of the way to Thailand. It took a few days.

We lived in Thailand for about five years, waiting to go to the United States. In Thailand people made houses from wood. We went to classes to learn English. We learned about what kind of food people ate in the U.S., what kinds of money they had, and how to use money. They taught us about how to dress in the United States, how so many things were different from Cambodian ways.

Finally we came to New York. I went to Roosevelt High School. I was fourteen years old then. I cried every single day I went to school. Everyone

33

The result of Pol Pot's efforts to increase rice production for export was an increase in the number of Cambodians who starved.

laughed at my clothes because they didn't look right. They didn't like me because I couldn't talk right, my English was so bad. I missed so many classes because I was always crying. It was very bad. Later I went to English classes at night to get my diploma. I'm almost done with classes. Soon I'll graduate. I want to get a job.

I take care of my parents and grandparents. They don't work anymore since we came here. They are too old. They are very strict and do everything the Cambodian way. They don't want me to go out of the house. I only go out to my classes. If I get a job and go out, my English will get better and I will meet people.

I don't miss Cambodia because it was so bad there. Mostly all I remember is the war and working hard and always being very hungry. Now I want to be an American.◆

Thol has been in the United States since 1985. He was very young during the war in Cambodia and doesn't remember much about his life there. Thol's family left Cambodia in 1982 and stayed in a Thai refugee camp for a little over two years.

He seems happy here in the U.S., though he is also proud of his Cambodian heritage and very much wants to return for a visit to his country. He meets with other Cambodian teens at a youth group in Dallas. Thol is now sixteen years old.

THOL
IT'S MY CULTURE

When we left Cambodia there was no work. In the camp we went to there was one time during the day when you had to line up to get food and water. We were there for two years.

Before we could leave the camp, my parents had to have their application to leave accepted. In Cambodia my dad worked as a butcher. Now he works fixing people's houses. My mom sells stuff on the street corner. She sells vegetables from the garden. We have a really big front yard where we can grow corn and other vegetables.

At home we still speak Cambodian. My aunt has been back to Cambodia three times since we came here. She has all these statues of dancers. I'm a Christian. I think I'm the only one in my family. I'm different from everyone. They still go to the Buddhist temple and all that. I go too, but just to make my mom happy.

Thousands of Cambodians packed up whatever belongings they could carry and fled to refugee camps in Thailand.

Traditional Cambodian Dress

Traditional Cambodian dress is similar to that of India. Most Cambodians now wear Western-type clothes or simple black Chinese pajamas as a uniform to work in the countryside. Some of the more exotic and interesting articles of traditional dress are listed below. These items are now worn for ceremonial occasions such as weddings and New Year's celebrations.

The *sampot* is a piece of silk or cotton cloth wrapped around the waist with the longest piece brought between the legs and then tucked into or attached at the waist. The *sampot*, usually worn by men, looks like a pair of puffed-out pants. Fabrics may be intricately batiked patterns in brilliant colors, or gold or silver brocades, as well as simple bright colors.

The Malay *sarong* is the main garment worn by women. It consists of a piece of silk or cotton cloth wrapped at the waist like a skirt. It is topped by a short-sleeved, short-waisted shirt. Both pieces are usually made of brilliantly colored or batik-patterned and brocaded fabrics. Both men and women have traditionally worn loosely tied turbans.

Coming here to the U.S., you have lots of opportunity. You have free education. There is not much education back in Cambodia. I came over here with my mom, dad, two older sisters, and one younger brother. My younger sister was born here. My aunt and cousin came too. I have an uncle back in Cambodia and a whole lot of family. I don't know any of them, but my dream is to go back to see Cambodia. Now I just want to graduate, to have a good job.

Dance

The National Ballet was once attached to the royal palace. It was a famous troupe of highly skilled dancers who performed dances expressing the rich stories of Cambodian folklore as well as the great myths of India. During the regime of Pol Pot, dancers were among the many artists who were persecuted. Of two hundred in the troupe in the 1975, only seventeen survived those terrible years. Pol Pot's own sister was a respected teacher of dance as far back as the 1940s. As one of the surviving members of the National Ballet, she helped train new teachers who have retrained a new troupe of dancers. The dances are long, complex, and require many years of study to perform expertly. One of the interesting differences between Cambodian ballet and the ballet style of the West is the expressive way the hands and feet are used. Costumes are elaborate, brilliantly colored, and often accented with gold and silver. Dance has long been part of Buddhist celebrations and is an important element in Cambodian traditions.

Cambodian music and dance is kind of weird. It's from the temple. At the temple, you dance and you move your fingers around. You wear really beautiful costumes. On New Year's I did a Cambodian dance. Some guys over here are shy and don't want to do it. But I figure, what the heck, it's my culture, I'll do it.◆

Khmer dance is a combination of complex movements including the hands and feet.

Debbie's family came to the United States in 1984. She was four years old then. She is very happy and settled in her life in Dallas.

DEBBIE
CAMBODIAN NEW YEAR

4

Things in Cambodia were very bad. My dad was a soldier. We left for Thailand. We lived there for three or four months, then we went to the Philippines. We lived there for about a year. Then we went to Hong Kong for a while before coming to the United States.

On special occasions we make Cambodian foods. We have to have rice every day, but we don't eat Cambodian foods all the time. My very favorite Cambodian food is a soup. It has green watercress and some fish, maybe catfish. With some salt and sugar and black pepper, that's about it. That's a regular food, not a special thing. It takes a long time just to make a Cambodian meal.

Cambodian New Year

Cambodian New Year is celebrated in the middle of April. It is the most important Buddhist holiday of the year, celebrated by almost all Cambodians, even those who have moved away from Cambodia and embraced other religions. The traditional celebration includes the creation of small piles of sand to represent the great mountains of Hindu teachings. Mount Meru, home of the Hindu gods, is the most important of these.

For centuries this ceremony was performed in the Silver Pagoda of the Royal Palace in Phnom Penh at the same time that monks in monasteries and humble villagers in their own homes celebrated. It was a day when everyone feasted, wore their finest clothing, played games, sang songs, and danced. All of Cambodia rejoiced on this day called Cul Chnam Tigey.

Many Cambodian parents are very strict. I can't go out at all. No boys can call. I'm not really allowed to have any guy friends. My parents wouldn't know if I had friends at school, but I would never give a boy my phone number.

I go to Buddhist temple on holidays. The most important holiday is probably Cambodian New Year, April 13, 14, 15. Usually we don't go to school on those days. Instead we go to temple and have fun, play games, traditional Cambodian games like tug of war, *teanh proath* in Cambodian. We dress up in fancy clothes, bright colors, fabrics with really fancy patterns.

Someday I'd like to go back to Cambodia. I'm the youngest child in the family, the fifth one. My

Traditional Cambodian costumes are vivid with intricate beadwork and vibrant colors.

Fish: A Favorite Food

Fish is a favorite food of many Cambodians. Along with rice, *prahoc,* a delicious fermented fish paste is a regular part of the Cambodian diet. Traditionally *prahoc* is prepared on the banks of the Tonle Sap river. In November during the full moon, the current in the river flowing out of the lake reverses. The fish then rush downstream, where Cambodians have built dams to trap tremendous quantities. As the fish are pulled out of the river, some are quickly scaled and gutted. Then they are washed, dried, and salted. The juice that comes to the surface of the fish paste is called Cambodian brine and is also used as a condiment for traditional foods.

---

mom and my older brother came over here. My older sisters, two of them and a brother, all died. It was while we were trying to escape, because of hunger, I think. I was so young I guess it didn't really affect me. I was only four months old when we left. I never knew what my dad looked like. I imagine if I went back to Cambodia I wouldn't know how things work over there. I'm just so used to everything here.◆

Signs of the brutal reign of Pol Pot's Khmer Rouge are reflected in all aspects of Cambodian culture. Here they are depicted in a painting.

Sammy has only been in the United States for six years. He is the youngest in a large family. He lived in Cambodia until his family moved to the United States. Long Beach, California, the community where Sammy lives, has one of the largest Cambodian populations in the U.S., with as many as 50,000 Cambodians living in the area.

SAMMY
SOMETIMES THE LANDMINES
KILL YOU

My family wanted to leave Cambodia for a long time. We had to wait for some relatives to send us money. When our relatives saved enough they sent for us. One older sister and two older brothers left first. I had another brother who had to go into the army. We never saw him again. I don't know what happened to him. Soldiers just came to get people. I was afraid my other brother would be taken, but he went to the United States instead. Then my grandmother and father and I were able to come. The trip took a long time. We went on three different planes. I have another sister who stayed in Cambodia with her husband's family. They didn't want to come to the U.S.

Officials have begun to remove the thousands of landmines laid
during the civil war in the 1970s.

My mother died in an accident in Cambodia. My brother limps because his foot got hurt by a land-mine that soldiers put in the fields. Sometimes those mines kill you. Sometimes they only take away your hand or something. I wish my mother could have come to the U.S. with us. She would have liked it.

When first we came here I didn't think it would be good. Everything was noisy and fast. I still don't like American food. School here is hard. At first I was afraid at school. In Cambodia I didn't go to school very often. Schools closed down one day,

Landmines still remain from the civil war. Walking through fields or the jungle can be very dangerous. Even today many people are killed or lose a limb because of landmines.

opened another day. We moved to places where there was no school. Then my mother tried to teach me, but I only wanted to play and run around with my friends.

I work hard in school here and I made some friends. I have friends who come from Cambodia like me. Some of them are my cousins, too. Most of them came here a long time ago so they speak English better than me and they know more about things. They tell me when I say things wrong or if my clothes don't look right, stuff like that. I have American friends, but they don't understand me

Refugees are often forced to leave relatives behind. Sometimes it is possible to maintain contact; other times it is not.

as well.

I sometimes miss Cambodia. I miss my sister who stayed there. Sometimes she writes me letters. She has a little baby so I am an uncle now. I hope I get to see her again one day.◆

Ban was only four years old when she came to the United States in 1985. Her little brother was two. Ban and her brother were both born in Thailand, but her family is from Cambodia. A church group helped them and some other families get to the U.S. and found host families for them for several months. The host families helped the Cambodians look for jobs and apartments. Eventually the Cambodians, Ban's family among them, were able to move out on their own and begin a new life in the U.S. Ban is now thirteen years old.

6

BAN
BORN IN A REFUGEE CAMP

I was born when my parents were living in a refugee camp in Thailand. I've never even been to Cambodia, but I still think of myself as being Cambodian, and American too. My grandmother lives in Cambodia. We are going to visit her next year. She stayed with my uncle and aunt, but they died before I was born. Now she takes care of my cousins who live there too.

My parents decided it would be better to leave Cambodia because there was no food and no one could do anything unless the government said so. My father used to be an engineer. My mother was a teacher. They lived in an apartment in the city. It was dangerous for them because the Khmer Rouge, who won the war, took over everything and killed lots of people who had worked in the city, who

The Khmer Rouge were brutal in their tactics. As a result, thousands of people died. This sixteen-year-old girl holds snapshots of herself and her family. She was the only family member to survive.

were educated. My parents were lucky they didn't get killed. But they were forced to leave the city and go work on farms planting rice. They weren't even able to stay together on the same farm. Then they decided to leave Cambodia.

I was born in a refugee camp and so was my little brother. We were there for a long time, almost six years. I only remember a little about it. I didn't know I was in a camp or anything. If I think about it hard, I can sort of remember that it was kind of noisy and crowded with lots of other people like us, Cambodians, everywhere. That seems kind of strange now because it's so different in the U.S. and I'm used to being here.

Most of what I remember is about my life in the U.S. I don't even remember coming here. One thing I remember about the place we stayed when we first came here is the toys the people we stayed with gave us. I never had really nice toys like that, so I guess that's why I remember. I got a Barbie doll and some stuffed animals that I really loved. The mother in the family also taught me to play "Twinkle, Twinkle Little Star" on the piano.

I don't remember learning how to speak English. It wasn't very hard for me. My brother learned English before he could even speak Cambodian. He still can't speak Cambodian very well and he gets mad at the rest of us if we talk too fast and he doesn't know what we're saying. It's very funny. I speak Cambodian with my parents so that I won't forget. My mother still doesn't speak

Refugees in Thailand lived in small, cramped quarters. This thirteen-year-old boy kneels on his bed in a six-foot cubicle in a thatched-roof bamboo hut that houses him and four other family members.

English too well. My father got a job working in a place that makes copies and sends faxes. He fixes machines and stuff like that. He speaks English almost as well as I do. My mom stays at home with us. She wants to get a job when her English is better.

There are a lot of Asian kids in my school so I didn't feel strange or different really. Nobody treated me like an outsider. For a while I was embarrassed that my parents were different, celebrating Cambodian holidays, and stuff like that. I thought they were so strict and not as nice as other kids' parents.

Now I think I'm more interested in my Cambodian background than I was before. It's hard to imagine my father and mother working in rice fields or running away through the jungle, but they did. I think that they are very brave people. When I think about that, it makes me proud that I am Cambodian. I'm looking forward to visiting there.◆

Glossary

abdicate To give up formally, as the right to a throne or power.

archaeologist Scientist who studies the life and culture of past peoples by excavating ancient cities, relics, and artifacts.

batik Method of dyeing a design on clothing by coating with removable wax the parts not to be dyed.

brocade Rich cloth with a raised design woven into it.

Buddhism Religion popular in some Asian countries, which teaches that the ideal state is reached by right living and meditation.

communism Political system in which there is no private property or industry.

execution Putting to death according to a legally imposed sentence.

figurehead Person holding himself as a leader but having no power or authority.

flood plain Expanse of land bordering on a river and frequently flooded when the river rises high.

genocide The intentional and systematic killing of an entire people or national group.

Hinduism A religion of India, whose god is Brahma; its followers pursue mystical practices.

isolation National policy calling for self-sufficiency and avoidance of ties with foreign countries.

Khmer Member of an ancient people of Cambodia.

landmine Explosive device buried where people are likely to step on it and set it off, causing death or serious injury.

monsoon Seasonal wind of the Pacific that frequently brings flooding rains.

observatory Place for the systematic study of the heavens and the movements of the stars and planets.

orphanage An institution housing children who do not have parents.

peninsula Body of land almost surrounded by water and connected to the mainland by an isthmus.

starvation Suffering or becoming weak from severe hunger.

For Further Reading

Bailie, Allan. *Little Brother*. New York: Viking
    Children's Books, 1992.
Canesso, Claudia. *Cambodia*. New York:
    Chelsea House Publishers, 1989.
Chandler, David P. *The Land and People of
    Cambodia*. New York: HarperCollins, 1991.
Howard, Richard. *Where the River Runs:
    Portrait of a Refugee Family*. Boston: Little,
    Brown & Company, 1993.

Also of Interest:
The Killing Fields. Movie based on the
    experiences of Cambodian photojournalist
    Dith Pran, produced in 1984.
Cambodian Doughnut Dreams. Documentary
    film about how a community of Cambodians
    have adjusted to life in the U.S.

Index

About the Author

Stephanie St. Pierre is the author of more than forty books for children, including *Jim Henson, Creator of the Muppets* and *Everything You Need to Know When a Parent Is In Jail.* Currently she is working on a children's novel, several pop-up books, and stories for children to be produced in television and film.

Ms. St. Pierre lives in Brooklyn, New York, with her husband, two children, and a big black dog named Shadow. Someday she would like to visit Cambodia to see Angkor Wat.

Photo Credits

cover, p. 51 © Leah Melnick/Impact Visuals; p. 11, 15, 19, 52 © Tom and Michele Grimm/Int'l Stock Photo; p. 16, 41, 45 © John Elbers/Int'l Stock Photo; pp. 32, 47 © Sean Sprague/Impact Visuals; all other photos © AP/Wide World Photos

Layout and Design

Kim Sonsky